DIGITAL CITIZENSHIP
FACTS AND OPINIONS

by Kristine Spanier, MLIS

po go

Ideas for Parents and Teachers

Pogo Books let children practice reading informational text while introducing them to nonfiction features such as headings, labels, sidebars, maps, and diagrams, as well as a table of contents, glossary, and index.

Carefully leveled text with a strong photo match offers early fluent readers the support they need to succeed.

Before Reading

- "Walk" through the book and point out the various nonfiction features. Ask the student what purpose each feature serves.
- Look at the glossary together. Read and discuss the words.

Read the Book

- Have the child read the book independently.
- Invite him or her to list questions that arise from reading.

After Reading

- Discuss the child's questions. Talk about how he or she might find answers to those questions.
- Prompt the child to think more. Ask: Can you provide a piece of information that is a fact? What about an opinion?

Pogo Books are published by Jump!
5357 Penn Avenue South
Minneapolis, MN 55419
www.jumplibrary.com

Library of Congress Cataloging-in-Publication Data

Names: Spanier, Kristine, author.
Title: Facts and opinions / by Kristine Spanier.
Description: Minneapolis, MN: Pogo Books, 2019.
Series: Digital citizenship | Includes index.
Identifiers: LCCN 2018032147 (print)
LCCN 2018043725 (ebook)
ISBN 9781641284400 (ebook)
ISBN 9781641284387 (hardcover: alk. paper)
ISBN 9781641284394 (pbk.)
Subjects: LCSH: Media literacy–Juvenile literature.
Classification: LCC P96.M4 (ebook) | LCC P96.M4 S65 2019 (print) | DDC 302.23–dc23
LC record available at https://lccn.loc.gov/2018032147

Editor: Jenna Trnka
Designer: Michelle Sonnek

Photo Credits: goir/Shutterstock, cover (left); Luchenko Yana/Shutterstock, cover (right); Jane Kelly/Shutterstock, 1; scanrail/iStock, 3; Everett - Art/Shutterstock, 4; Mark Wilson/Getty, 5; kzenon/iStock, 6–7; Luciano Mortula - LGM/Shutterstock, 8–9; blickwinkel/Alamy, 10; K Hanley CHDPhoto/Shutterstock, 11; Kaspars Grinvalds/Shutterstock, 12–13 (background); giulio napolitano/Shutterstock, 12–13 (Pope Francis); Drop of Light/Shutterstock, 12–13 (Donald Trump); Africa Studio/Shutterstock, 14–15 (background); AP Images, 14–15 (TV screen); ibrandify gallery/Shutterstock, 16; phatcharin maungngarm/Shutterstock, 17 (background); Ermolaev Alexander/Shutterstock, 17 (billboard); lev radin/Shutterstock, 18–19; 8213erika/iStock, 20–21 (background); AveNa/Shutterstock, 20 (TV screen); DNY59/iStock, 23.

Printed in the United States of America at Corporate Graphics in North Mankato, Minnesota.

TABLE OF CONTENTS

CHAPTER 1

MANY MESSAGES

George Washington was the first U.S. president. Is that a fact? Yes.

George Washington was the best president. Is that a fact? No. That is an opinion.

A fact is information that can be proven. How? Through historic record. Research from experts. Or news reported by fair **journalists**.

Opinions are beliefs. What flavor of ice cream is the best? What makes a great leader? No one can tell you what to believe.

We need to know the difference between fact and opinion. How can we do this? We can ask questions. Who created the information? Why?

DID YOU KNOW?

Every day, we may see or hear up to 100,000 words! Some of them are facts. Many are opinions. We see as much information in one day as a person in the 1400s saw in a lifetime.

CHAPTER 2

FAKE AND BIASED NEWS

In 2018, an alarming news story spread on **social media**. A spider new to the United States had bitten five people. They died.

NEW DEADLY SPIDER SPREADS ACROSS USA

The images showed a woodlouse spider. It is not new to the country. Its bite cannot kill humans. No one had died due to this spider. The story was fake news.

Pope Francis Shocks World, Endorses Donald Trump For President

Fake news is made to look like facts. Some is made to make certain leaders look more popular. In 2016, a website said Pope Francis had **endorsed** Donald Trump as president. This was not true. But the website looked like a real news site. People were tricked.

Some news sources are **conservative**. FOX News is one. It **criticizes** leaders from the Democratic Party. It praises the Republican Party. MSNBC is more **liberal**. It criticizes Republican leaders more. This is called **biased** news.

WHAT DO YOU THINK?

Some people create **blogs** to deliver fake news. Or to present biased information. They want people to agree with their opinions. Do you think this is OK? Why or why not?

OCASIO-CORTEZ ON THE FAMILY SEPARATION CRISIS

LIVE
MSNBC
6:41 AM MT

CHAPTER 3

ADVERTISING

Advertisements, or ads, used to only be in magazines. Newspapers. Radio. TV. The Internet changed this. Now they are on websites and social media. In apps and games, too.

Ads are a mix of fact and opinion. Companies use them to get you to buy products or services. Like what? Cars. Soft drinks. Fast food. They may use cute animals to get your attention.

An actor might hold a certain brand of soda in a TV show or movie. Or drive a certain car. This is called **product placement**. Have you seen **logos** on an athlete's clothing? Companies pay money for this. Why? So people see it and want to buy that product or service.

WHAT DO YOU THINK?

Native advertising looks like news. Different phrases are used on native ads. Like what? Paid Advertisement. Presented by. Have you noticed these before? Did you know this was advertising?

logo

NOTICE

WEAR A SEAT BELT

Pro bono ads are public service messages. They tell us to make healthy choices. Like what? Wear a seat belt. Don't litter. Don't smoke. Do you think these messages work? Why or why not?

Learn the differences between facts and opinions. Know when a company is trying to sell you something. This will help you make better decisions.

TAKE A LOOK!

Companies often use opinion statements in their ads. Why? These make you buy things you may not need. Do you notice the difference between fact and opinion in these statements?

Fact vs. Opinion

Fact		Opinion
These shoes are made of leather and rubber.	→	These shoes will make you run faster.
This gum has a mint flavor.	→	You need to have fresh breath.
Our burgers cost $1.	→	Our burgers taste better.
You can schedule a birthday party at our ninja gym on Saturdays.	→	Your birthday party will be more fun at a ninja gym.
This toothpaste can reduce teeth stains.	→	Your teeth look better when they are white.

ACTIVITIES & TOOLS

FACT-CHECK INFORMATION

Pay attention to news you see or hear. Do some research to find out if it is true. How? Follow the steps below. Is the information fake?

❶ If the information is online, what website is it on? Reliable sources usually end in .edu (educational institutions), .gov (U.S. government), or .org (organizations).

❷ Check multiple sources. Can you find the same story on a trusted news site? NPR.org is an example. So is reuters.com.

❸ Does the story have a poll or survey? Who conducted it? How many people were asked? How were they picked? Was it fair or biased?

❹ Is the headline just a little too funny or scary? This is known as clickbait. It is probably fake. The person who created it gets money if you click on the link.

❺ Does the story warn you of a future disaster? Disasters can't be predicted.

❻ Look for the story on fact-checking sites. One trusted site is www.factcheck.org.

biased: Favoring one person or point of view more than another.

blogs: Websites that contain personal opinions, comments, videos, and photographs provided by the writer.

conservative: In favor of smaller government and businesses and opposed to large social welfare programs.

criticizes: Evaluates someone and tells that person he or she has done or is doing something wrong, often in a hostile way.

endorsed: To have shown support or approval of someone or something.

journalists: Writers or editors for news media.

liberal: In favor of political change and reform.

logos: Distinctive symbols or trademarks that identify a particular company or organization.

native advertising: Ads on an online publication that look like the publication's content but are paid for by advertisers to promote their products.

pro bono: Involving doing work for free.

product placement: When a company pays to place a product so viewers will see it in a TV show or movie.

social media: Forms of electronic communication through which users create and share information.

INDEX

TO LEARN MORE

Finding more information is as easy as 1, 2, 3.

1 Go to www.factsurfer.com

2 Enter "factsandopinions" into the search box.

3 Click the "Surf" button to see a list of websites.

FACT SURFER